A Comprehensive Galaxy S24 & S24 plus User Manual

The Essential Guide to AI features and softwares, DeX, SmartThings, features, tips, tricks and More

Composed By

Shondel Cotella

Table of content

Chapter 1: Welcome to the Galaxy S24: A Universe of Possibilities at Your Fingertips

Step into a world of cutting-edge technology and boundless potential with the Samsung Galaxy S24. This isn't just a phone; it's a gateway to a universe of possibilities, crafted with your every need in mind.

Experience Unmatched Brilliance: Immerse yourself in a visual feast on the Galaxy S24's stunning Dynamic AMOLED 2X display. Whether you're browsing breathtaking landscapes, streaming your favorite shows, or conquering intense games, vibrant colors and unparalleled clarity come alive before your eyes. Every pixel glistens with life, ensuring a viewing experience that's as smooth as it is captivating.

Unleash the Power Within: At the heart of the Galaxy S24 beats the next generation of Samsung's Exynos 8900 processor, pushing the boundaries of performance and efficiency. Multitask with ease between demanding apps, experience seamless gameplay without lag, and witness lightning-fast response times at every touch. This powerhouse processor ensures you'll never compromise on speed or power, keeping pace with your ambitions.

Capture the Extraordinary: Elevate your photography to new heights with the Galaxy S24's revolutionary camera system. Boasting a multi-lens array powered by AI, capture stunning landscapes with breathtaking detail, bring portraits to life with expert clarity, and freeze fleeting moments in mesmerizing sharpness. AI Scene Optimizer and Shot Suggestions intelligently adjust settings for perfect results, while advanced low-light capabilities let you capture the magic even in the darkest corners.

Intelligence that Amplifies You: Introducing Bixby, your ever-evolving personal assistant. Go beyond the limitations of voice commands and experience true conversational interaction. Bixby anticipates your needs, learns your preferences, and proactively assists you throughout your day. Whether it's booking appointments, controlling your smart home, or finding the perfect playlist, Bixby is your intelligent sidekick, always a step ahead.

A Universe Just for You: The Galaxy S24 transcends the boundaries of just a phone. It's a customizable canvas for your personality and passions. With an intuitive interface and endless personalization options, tailor your experience to your unique style. From vibrant themes and custom widgets to intuitive gestures and seamless integrations, the Galaxy S24 is an extension of you, reflecting your individuality in every way.

The Galaxy S24 is more than just a device; it's an invitation to explore, create, and connect. It's a universe of possibilities waiting to be unlocked, nestled comfortably in the palm of your hand. Take the first step into a world of wonder and experience the extraordinary with the Samsung Galaxy S24.

Chapter 2:Unboxing Your Galaxy S24: A Journey Begins

With anticipation buzzing, gently remove the sleek outer packaging of your Galaxy S24. Within, nestled in a protective embrace, lies your technological companion, ready to embark on a journey with you.

As you lift the phone, admire its refined design. The premium materials and flawless craftsmanship reflect Samsung's dedication to quality. Run your fingers along the smooth contours, appreciating the ergonomic fit that promises effortless one-handed use.

Beneath the phone, you'll find a treasure trove of essential accessories:

* **Charging adapter:** Power up your Galaxy S24 with this quick-charging adapter for speedy refuels.
* **USB-C cable:** Connect your phone to your computer or charging adapter for seamless data transfer and power.
* **Earphones:** Immerse yourself in crystal-clear audio with these comfortable earphones, perfect for calls and entertainment.
* **SIM card ejector tool:** Access your SIM card slot with ease using this small but essential tool.
* **Quick Start Guide:** Get acquainted with the basics of your phone through this concise guide.

Optional accessories (depending on your model) might include:

* **Protective case:** Shield your Galaxy S24 from everyday bumps and scratches with a stylish and sturdy case.
* **Wireless charger:** Experience the convenience of cable-free charging with a sleek wireless charging pad.

Before venturing further, we recommend exploring some initial setup steps:

* **Insert your SIM card:** Locate the SIM card slot using the ejector tool and carefully insert your SIM card, following the on-screen instructions.
* **Charge your phone:** Connect the charging adapter and cable to your Galaxy S24, ensuring the battery has enough juice for the exciting journey ahead.
* **Turn it on:** Hold down the power button and witness the vibrant AMOLED display come to life. Follow the on-screen prompts to complete the initial setup process.

With these preliminaries completed, you're ready to delve deeper into the wonders of your Galaxy S24. The next steps involve connecting to Wi-Fi, setting up your Google account, and unlocking the full potential of your new companion.

Chapter3: Inserting the SIM card and microSD card: Unlocking Connectivity and Storage

Now that your Galaxy S24 is powered on and you've admired its sleek design, it's time to unlock its connectivity and storage capabilities. This involves inserting your SIM card and, if desired, a microSD card for additional storage space.

Finding the Slots:

Locate the SIM card tray on the side of your phone. Depending on your model, it might be located near the top or bottom. You can easily identify it by the small indentation or symbol indicating a tray.

SIM Card Insertion:

Using the provided SIM card ejector tool (a small metal pin), gently press the hole next to the tray until it pops out. Carefully place your SIM card into the designated slot, aligning the gold contacts with the corresponding pins on the tray. Ensure the cut corner of the card matches the angled corner of the slot.

MicroSD Card (Optional):

If you desire extra storage space, your Galaxy S24 might also have a dedicated microSD card slot. The location and insertion process are similar to the SIM card, just look for the microSD card symbol on the tray.

Pushing the Tray Back:

Once the cards are correctly positioned, gently push the tray back into its slot until it clicks securely shut.

Your phone will automatically recognize the cards and activate them, prompting you to set up your network connection and potentially download updates.

Troubleshooting Tips:

* If the tray doesn't eject easily, double-check you're pressing the ejector tool in the correct direction.
* Ensure the SIM card is properly aligned and inserted firmly into the slot.
* If your phone doesn't recognize the card, try restarting it or gently removing and reinserting the card.

These simple steps will unlock your Galaxy S24's communication and storage potential, paving the way for a connected and expansive mobile experience. Feel free to ask if you encounter any difficulties or need further guidance.

Chapter 4: Charging Your Galaxy S24: Powering Up for Possibilities

With your SIM card and microSD card in place, it's time to energize your Galaxy S24 for its first adventure. This sleek device boasts a powerful battery and intelligent charging technology, ensuring you always have the juice to fuel your activities.

Fueling for the Journey:

* **Connect the adapter:** Locate the USB-C port on the bottom of your phone. Plug the provided charging adapter into a wall outlet.
* **Connect the cable:** Attach the USB-C cable to the adapter and then to your phone's USB-C port. Ensure the connection is secure.
* **Witness the awakening:** Observe the LED indicator on your phone. When it lights up, your Galaxy S24 is receiving power.

Fast and Intelligent Charging:

* **Experience Super Fast Charging:** The Galaxy S24 boasts Samsung's Super Fast Charging technology, promising rapid battery replenishment. In just minutes, you can get enough power to tackle your day or charge up for a quick movie session.
* **Adaptive Battery Care:** The phone's Adaptive Battery Care learns your usage patterns and optimizes charging accordingly, extending the battery's lifespan and preventing overcharging.

Wireless Charging (Optional):

* **Unleash the freedom:** If you have a compatible wireless charging pad, you can ditch the cables and experience the convenience of wireless charging. Simply place your Galaxy S24 on the pad, and watch the battery level rise effortlessly.

Charging Tips for Optimal Performance:

* Use the provided charger and cable: For optimal performance and safety, utilize the accessories included with your phone.
* Avoid extreme temperatures: Don't charge your phone in excessively hot or cold environments.
* Update your software: Regularly update your phone's software to benefit from the latest battery optimization features.

With these tips in mind, you can ensure your Galaxy S24 stays powered up and ready to accompany you on every adventure.

Chapter 5: Turning on Your Galaxy S24 for the First Time: Unveiling a World of Potential

With your Galaxy S24 charged and ready to go, it's time to unveil the universe of possibilities it holds within. Prepare yourself for a delightful first encounter, an introduction to the technology that will become your trusted companion.

Awakening the Power:

1. **Hold down the power button:** Locate the power button on the side of your phone, usually towards the top. Press and hold it for a few seconds until the vibrant AMOLED display flickers to life.

2. **Welcome to the fold:** Witness the stunning display light up with the welcoming Samsung logo, followed by the initial setup screens.

3. **Choose your language:** Select your preferred language from the displayed options. This will set the language for the on-screen instructions and menus.

4. **Connect to Wi-Fi:** Select a Wi-Fi network and enter the password if necessary. Connecting to Wi-Fi allows you to download software updates and access online services.

First Steps on the Digital Path:

1. **Set up your Google account:** Enter your existing Google account credentials or create a new one. This unlocks access to Google Play Store, Gmail, Google Maps, and other essential Google services.

2. **Personalize your screen:** Choose your preferred wallpaper and theme, customizing the visual experience to your taste.

3. **Protect your world:** Set up a secure lock screen password or PIN to safeguard your data and privacy. You can choose from various options, including pattern lock, fingerprint unlock, or facial recognition.

4. **Meet Bixby, your AI companion:** Get acquainted with Bixby, your helpful assistant. Press and hold the Bixby button or say "Hi Bixby" to activate voice commands and explore all Bixby can do.

Ready to Dive Deeper:

Once you've completed these initial steps, you're ready to delve further into the exciting world of your Galaxy S24. Explore the pre-installed apps, download additional ones from the Play Store, and familiarize yourself with the navigation gestures and features.

Absolutely! Let's move on to "Setting up your Galaxy S24 with Smart Switch". This section can guide users on seamlessly transferring data from their old phone (Android or iOS) to their new Galaxy S24.

Chapter 6:Setting up Your Galaxy S24 with Smart Switch: A Seamless Transition

With your first steps on your Galaxy S24 complete, it's time to bring your memories and essentials along without breaking a sweat. Samsung's Smart Switch app makes transferring data from your old phone (Android or iOS) to your new Galaxy S24 a breeze. Let's dive in!

Preparing for the Switch:

* **Install Smart Switch:** Download and install the Smart Switch app on both your old and new phones.

You can find it on the Google Play Store for Android devices and the App Store for iOS devices.

* **Ensure Wi-Fi connection:** Both phones need to be connected to the same Wi-Fi network for the transfer to work.

* **Prepare your old phone:** Ensure your old phone has sufficient battery life and is unlocked. If required, update the software to the latest version for best compatibility.

Making the Switch:

1. **Launch Smart Switch on both phones:** Open the Smart Switch app on both devices.

2. **Choose transfer method:** On your new Galaxy S24, select "Receive data" as the transfer mode. On your old phone, select "Send data" or choose the relevant option for your device model.

3. **Connect the phones:** Choose your preferred connection method. You can connect wirelessly via Wi-Fi Direct or use a USB cable (not included, check if your old phone uses the same connector type as your new Galaxy S24).

4. **Select content to transfer:** On your old phone, choose the data you want to transfer, such as

contacts, photos, videos, music, messages, and apps. You can select everything or choose specific items.

5. **Start the transfer**: Tap "Transfer" or "Start" on both phones to begin the process. The transfer time will vary depending on the amount of data being transferred.

6. **Set up your Galaxy S24:** Once the transfer is complete, follow the remaining on-screen setup instructions on your new Galaxy S24. This might include setting up your Google account, choosing a lock screen method, and downloading additional apps.

Tips for a smooth transition:

* Close any open apps on both phones before starting the transfer.
* Ensure both phones have sufficient storage space available for the incoming data.
* Have your charging cables handy in case the battery level gets low on either phone during the transfer.
* If you encounter any issues during the transfer, be sure to check the Smart Switch app for troubleshooting tips or contact Samsung customer support.

With Smart Switch, transitioning to your new Galaxy S24 is a seamless and stress-free experience. You can now enjoy all your cherished memories and essential data on your new device, ready to embark on new adventures.

Chapter 7: Transferring data from your old phone: Alternative Routes

While Smart Switch is often the quickest and easiest way to migrate data from your old phone, there are other options for those who might prefer alternative methods. This section will explore some additional transfer possibilities:

1. Google Drive Backup:

- Backup your contacts, photos, videos, and other data from your old phone to Google Drive.
- During the initial setup of your Galaxy S24, sign in with your Google account and choose to restore previously backed-up data.

2. Samsung Cloud:

- Similar to Google Drive, back up your data to Samsung Cloud on your old phone.
- During setup on your Galaxy S24, sign in with your Samsung account and restore your backed-up data.

3. PC/Mac Transfer:

- Use Samsung's Smart Switch program on your computer to back up your old phone data.
- Connect your Galaxy S24 to your computer and transfer the data back using Smart Switch.

4. Manual File Transfer:

- Connect your old phone and Galaxy S24 using a USB cable.
- Access the files on your old phone and manually copy them to the desired folders on your Galaxy S24.

5. **Third-party apps:**

- Various third-party apps offer data transfer between phones, potentially supporting additional data types or offering specific features.

Choosing the Right Method:

- Consider the data you want to transfer (contacts, photos, messages, apps, etc.) and the amount of data involved.
- Evaluate your comfort level with technology and whether you prefer a wireless or wired approach.
- Choose the method that best suits your needs and technical expertise.

Chapter 8: Guarding Your Galaxy's Gateway

Securing your Galaxy S24 with a lock screen pattern or PIN is a crucial step in safeguarding your personal information and data. This section will guide you through the process of setting up and managing these security options, empowering you to protect your digital world.

Creating Your Secure Pattern

1. **Access the Settings menu:** Tap on the Settings icon (typically resembling a gear) from your Home screen or Apps screen.

2. **Find the Security menu:** Locate the Security menu within the Settings options.

3. **Choose lock screen method:** Tap on the "Lock screen" option and select either "Screen lock pattern" or "Screen lock PIN", depending on your preference.

4. **Set your pattern or PIN:** Follow the on-screen instructions to create your desired pattern or enter a secure PIN. Ensure you remember it!

5. **Verify your creation:** Re-create the pattern or enter the PIN again to confirm its accuracy.

Additional Security Options

* **Lock screen visibility:** Choose whether to display notifications on the lock screen for a balanced approach between security and accessibility.

* **Smart lock:** Enhance your security experience with features like Trusted face, Trusted voice, or Trusted places, which can automatically unlock your device under specific conditions.

* **Find My Mobile:** In case of loss or misplacement, this feature can assist in locating, locking, or erasing your device, protecting your data.

Modifying or Disabling Your Security

* **Change pattern or PIN:** Access the Security settings and tap on the "Screen lock" option to change your existing pattern or PIN.

* **Disable lock screen:** If you wish to remove the lock screen security, tap on the "Turn off screen lock" option. Exercise
caution before disabling security measures.

* **Regularly change patterns or PINs:** Enhance security by regularly changing your patterns or PINs for optimal protection.

* **Avoid public patterns:** Choose patterns that are not easily guessable or visible to others when you unlock your device.

Chapter 9: Getting to Know Your Galaxy S24: A Familiarization Tour

With your lock screen secure and ready to guard your digital world, it's time to embark on a guided tour of your Galaxy S24! This section will equip you with an insightful understanding of your device's physical components, key features, and essential operations.

Let's Navigate the Landscape:

* Front view: The vibrant AMOLED display takes center stage, flanked by slim bezels for an immersive viewing experience. Above the display, you'll find the earpiece and front-facing camera.
* Back view: Depending on your model, the back panel might boast a sleek glass or textured finish. The rear camera module, housing multiple lenses and a flash, adds a touch of sophisticated elegance.
* Sides: Locate the power button and volume buttons, typically positioned towards the right side. Some models might offer additional buttons like Bixby or camera keys.
* Top and bottom: On the top edge, you might find an IR blaster (depending on your model), while the bottom houses the USB-C port and speaker grille.

Unveiling the Interface:

* Home screen: This is your primary landing point, customizable with widgets, app icons, and shortcuts for instant access to your favorite features.
* Apps screen: Swipe upwards from the Home screen to access the Apps screen, housing all your installed applications alphabetically.
* Navigation bar: Located at the bottom of the display, the navigation bar houses virtual buttons for Back, Home, and Recent Apps.

Essential Gestures:

* Swiping: Swipe up to go Home, swipe left or right to switch between apps, and swipe down from the top to access the notification panel.
* Pinching: Pinch in or out to zoom in or out on photos, maps, and web pages.
* Long press: Long press on an app icon or Home screen element to access additional options or context menus.

Familiarizing with Features:

* **Camera:** Explore the versatile camera app, with various modes and settings to capture stunning photos and videos.
* **Gallery:** Organize and edit your captured memories within the Gallery app.
* **Bixby:** Your AI companion awaits! Press and hold the Bixby button or say "Hi Bixby" to activate voice commands and explore Bixby's vast capabilities.
* **Settings:** This comprehensive menu allows you to personalize your device, manage connections, configure security, and adjust various system settings.

Chapter 10: Home screen and navigation: Building Your Digital Oasis

The Home screen serves as your personal gateway to the world of your Galaxy S24. This section will empower you to personalize this central hub and navigate your device with ease, allowing you to access your favorite apps and features swiftly and intuitively.

Customizing Your Home:

* Add widgets: Place handy widgets on your Home screen for instant access to weather updates, news headlines, calendar events, or music controls. Long press on an empty space on the Home screen to access the Widgets menu.
* Change wallpapers and themes: Set a personalized wallpaper or explore a variety of themes to reflect your individual style and preferences. Tap and hold on an empty space on the Home screen to access these options.

* Organize apps:Create folders to group related apps for better organization. Drag and drop app icons onto each other to create folders.

* Move and resize icons: Long press on an app icon to access the move and resize options. Arrange your icons in a way that feels intuitive and convenient for you.

Mastering the Navigation:

* The virtual buttons: Familiarize yourself with the Back, Home, and Recent Apps buttons at the bottom of your display. Tap the Back button to go back one step, press the Home button to return to the main screen, and tap the Recent Apps button to view previously used apps.

* Gestures for enhanced control: Swipe up from the bottom to go Home, swipe left or right to switch between open apps, and swipe down from the top to access the notification panel. You can also activate additional gestures for specific functions, like launching apps or taking screenshots.

Quick Access at Your Fingertips:

* App Drawer: Swipe upwards from the Home screen to access the App Drawer, where all your installed apps are listed alphabetically. You can also search for specific apps through the search bar at the top.
* Notification panel: Swipe down from the top of the screen to access the notification panel. Here, you'll find notifications from various apps, system alerts, and quick settings for commonly used features like Wi-Fi, Bluetooth, and brightness.

Chapter 11:Notifications Panel: Your Gateway to Alerts and Shortcuts

The notifications panel on your Galaxy S24 acts as a bustling information hub, keeping you abreast of updates, alerts, and vital system information. This section will equip you with the knowledge to navigate this panel with ease and utilize its functionalities for enhanced productivity and convenience.

Accessing the Panel:

Simply swipe down from the top edge of your screen to reveal the notifications panel. It expands in two sections:

* Top section: Displays notifications from various apps and system alerts.
* Bottom section: Houses quick settings tiles for commonly used features like Wi-Fi, Bluetooth, brightness, airplane mode, and silent mode.

Managing Notifications:

* Individual actions: Tap on a notification to open the related app or perform specific actions (e.g., reply to a message, mark an email as read).
* Clear notifications: Swipe left or right on a notification to dismiss it individually. Tap the "Clear all" button at the bottom to remove all notifications at once.
* Priority notifications: Prioritize important notifications by swiping down on them and selecting "Priority." These notifications will stay at the top of the panel and appear even on the lock screen.

* Notification settings: Long press on a notification to access settings for that specific app's notifications. You can choose to block app notifications altogether, set notification priority, or adjust notification sounds and alerts.

Quick Settings Powerhouse:

* Tap on a quick setting tile: To activate or deactivate a feature like Wi-Fi or Bluetooth, simply tap on its tile.
* Long press on a tile: For deeper customization, long press on a quick setting tile. This might reveal additional options or launch related settings menus.
* Rearrange tiles: Keep your most-used settings at your fingertips by dragging and dropping the quick setting tiles to rearrange them in a preferred order.
* Add or remove tiles: Access the "Edit" option in the quick settings panel to add or remove specific tiles based on your needs and preferences.

Chapter 12: Quick Settings Panel: Mastering the Control Center of Your Galaxy S24

With the notifications panel conquered, let's level up your command with the mighty Quick Settings Panel. This customizable hub grants instant access to a plethora of system functions, offering a convenient way to personalize your experience and optimize your workflow.

Unlocking the Panel:

Simply swipe down twice from the top edge of your screen to unveil the full glory of the Quick Settings Panel. This expanded view grants access to a wider range of settings compared to the bottom section of the Notifications Panel.

Navigating the Tiles:

* Tap a tile:Activate or deactivate a feature like Wi-Fi, Bluetooth, or Flashlight with a single tap.
* Long press a tile: Explore deeper options or open dedicated settings menus for finer control. For

example, long-pressing the Wi-Fi tile might take you to the Wi-Fi network list.
* Swipe left or right: Scroll through the available tiles if they don't all fit on the screen.

Customizing Your Panel:

* Rearrange tiles: Drag and drop tiles to personalize the order and prioritize the settings you access most frequently.
* Add or remove tiles: Tap the "Edit" button (usually three dots or a gear icon) to access the tile management screen. Here, you can add or remove tiles based on your needs and preferences.
* Adjust brightness slider:Drag the brightness slider up or down to quickly adjust the screen's brightness.

Advanced Features:

* Create panels: You can create multiple Quick Settings panels for different situations. For example, you might have a "Work" panel with focus on

connectivity and productivity settings, and a "Relax" panel with media and gaming controls.

* Schedules and routines: Automate settings changes based on specific times or locations. For example, your Galaxy S24 can automatically turn on Wi-Fi when you arrive home or activate silent mode during bedtime hours.

I'm happy to hear you're interested in learning more about Bixby, your friendly AI assistant! Bixby can be a powerful tool for enhancing your Galaxy S24 experience, so let's dive into the world of voice commands and intelligent assistance.

Chapter 13: Bixby: Your Gateway to a World of Possibilities

Imagine having a personal helper always at your fingertips, ready to answer questions, complete tasks, and even control your smart home devices. That's the magic of Bixby, your Galaxy S24's built-in AI assistant. This section will equip you with the knowledge to activate Bixby, explore its capabilities, and discover how it can make your life easier and more productive.

Getting Started with Bixby:

There are three ways to awaken Bixby:

* Press and hold the Bixby button: Your Galaxy S24 might have a dedicated Bixby button on the side. Press and hold it for a few seconds to launch Bixby.
* Say "Hi Bixby": If your voice wake-up is enabled, simply say "Hi Bixby" to activate the assistant.
* Swipe diagonally from the bottom corner:On some models, you can swipe diagonally upwards from the bottom corner of the screen to launch Bixby.

What Can Bixby Do?

The possibilities are endless! Here are just a few examples of how Bixby can assist you:

* Set alarms and reminders: Never miss an important appointment or deadline again. Just tell

Bixby to set an alarm or reminder, and it will take care of it.

* Get information: Ask Bixby about the weather, news headlines, sports scores, or any other topic that comes to mind. It will search the web and provide you with concise and accurate answers.

* Control your device: Use Bixby voice commands to adjust the volume, take screenshots, launch apps, or open specific settings.

* Automate tasks: Create Bixby Routines to automate repetitive tasks like turning on your lights as you arrive home or playing music in the morning.

* Connect with your smart home: If you have compatible smart home devices, you can use Bixby to control them with your voice, such as turning on the lights, adjusting the thermostat, or locking the doors.

Learning and Growing:

The more you use Bixby, the smarter it becomes. It learns from your interactions and preferences, adapting to your needs and interests. So, don't be afraid to experiment with different commands and ask Bixby new questions!

Gestures at Your Fingertips:

Your Galaxy S24 understands a variety of gestures, each triggering specific actions for a seamless and intuitive experience. Let's explore the most common ones:

* Swiping:

* Swipe up from the bottom to go Home.
* Swipe left or right on the Home screen or within apps to switch between them.
* Swipe down from the top to access the notification panel.
* Swipe down again from the notification panel to access the Quick Settings Panel.

* Pinching:

* Pinch in or out on photos, maps, and web pages to zoom in or out.

* Long pressing:

* Long press on an app icon, Home screen element, or notification to access additional options or context menus.

* Additional gestures:

* Swipe diagonally up from the bottom corner to activate Bixby (on some models).
* Double-tap an empty space on the Home screen or Lock screen to turn on the screen (if enabled).
* Place your hand on the screen while the screen is on to mute calls and alarms.

Unlocking Gesture Potential:

* Explore Settings: Head to the Settings menu and navigate to "Advanced Features" or "Motion and gestures" to explore the full range of available gestures and fine-tune their settings.

* Practice makes perfect:Don't be discouraged if you don't master all gestures immediately. Practice makes perfect, so keep trying and soon you'll be navigating your Galaxy S24 with effortless finesse.
* Customization options: Some gestures, like double-tap to wake, can be disabled or reassigned to different functions. Tailor the gesture experience to your preferences for optimal comfort and control.

Chapter 14: Understanding Power Consumption:

* Identify battery hogs: Head to "Device care" in Settings and tap "Optimize now". This reveals apps draining the most battery. Consider restricting background activity or uninstalling rarely used apps.
* Display settings matter: Reduce screen brightness, enable auto-brightness, and set a shorter screen timeout to significantly improve battery life.
* Network impact: Wi-Fi and Bluetooth consume power. Disable them when not needed, and consider switching to mobile data only when necessary.

* Location services: GPS can be a battery drain. Disable location services for apps that don't require them constantly.

Smart Optimizations:

* Power saving mode: Activate this built-in mode for immediate battery savings by limiting background activity and reducing performance.
* Adaptive battery: This intelligent feature learns your usage patterns and prioritizes battery for frequently used apps.
* Sleep/auto-restart: Schedule your phone to sleep during nighttime or automatically restart at intervals to optimize battery performance.

Additional Tips:

* Keep software updated: Install the latest updates for your software and apps to benefit from battery-saving improvements.

* Avoid extreme temperatures: Hot and cold environments can degrade battery health. Keep your phone at moderate temperatures.
* Consider fast charging: If compatible, invest in a fast charger to quickly replenish your battery when needed.
* Monitor battery usage:Regularly check the "Battery" section in Settings to identify any abnormal power drains and adjust settings accordingly.

Fantastic choice! Unleashing the potential of your Galaxy S24's camera can be incredibly rewarding, opening doors to capturing breathtaking photos and videos. Whether you want to freeze vibrant moments, tell captivating stories, or experiment with artistic expression, your device is packed with features to empower your vision.

Chapter 15: Let's dive into the exciting world of your Galaxy S24's camera by exploring the three key pillars:

1. Shooting Modes:

* Auto Mode: Your go-to option for effortless capture in most situations. The camera analyzes the scene and automatically adjusts settings for optimal results.
* Pro Mode: For photography enthusiasts who want manual control. Adjust ISO, shutter speed, aperture, and white balance to achieve your desired artistic effects.
* Night Mode: Capture stunning details and vibrant colors even in low-light conditions. Ideal for nighttime landscapes, cityscapes, and indoor shots.
* Portrait Mode: Blur the background for professional-looking portraits that make your subject stand out. Perfect for close-ups of people, pets, or even captivating food shots.

* Food Mode: Enhance the visual appeal of your culinary creations with optimized colors and lighting. Ideal for food bloggers, Instagram foodies, or simply capturing special meals.

* Panorama Mode: Capture breathtaking landscapes, expansive cityscapes, or group shots by stitching together multiple images seamlessly.

* Super Slow-mo:Capture fleeting moments at ultra-high speeds, adding dramatic effects and emphasizing details you might miss at normal speed. Ideal for sports, action shots, or playful animal antics.

2. Mastering Settings:

* ISO: Controls the camera's sensitivity to light. Higher ISO values for capturing shots in low light, but introduce noise. Lower ISO for clear, crisp images in well-lit situations.

* Shutter Speed: Determines how long the camera sensor is exposed to light. Faster shutter speeds freeze action, while slower speeds blur movement and create light trails for artistic effects.

* Aperture: Controls the size of the opening that lets light into the camera, affecting depth of field. Wider aperture for blurry backgrounds and sharper subjects, while narrower aperture for sharper backgrounds and landscape shots.

* White Balance: Adjusts the color temperature of your image to match the lighting conditions. Choose from presets like "Daylight," "Cloudy," or "Tungsten" for accurate colors.

3. Pro Tips and Tricks:

* Composition: Rule of thirds, leading lines, and foreground elements can add visual interest and guide the viewer's eye.

* Lighting: Utilize natural light whenever possible, and experiment with shadows and highlights for dramatic effects.

* Focus: Tap on the screen to select a specific focus point for optimal sharpness.

* Editing: Enhance your photos and videos with built-in editing tools like filters, brightness adjustments, and cropping.

Connecting to other devices:

Your Galaxy S24 offers a plethora of ways to connect with the world around you, enhancing your audio experience, sharing files, and expanding your functionality. Here are some exciting possibilities:

* Pairing with headphones and speakers: Enjoy wireless audio freedom with Bluetooth headphones or earbuds. Elevate your music and movie nights by connecting to wireless speakers for immersive sound.
* Connecting to computers: Transfer files seamlessly between your Galaxy S24 and your computer via USB cable or Wi-Fi Direct. Use Samsung DeX mode to turn your phone into a desktop experience when connected to a monitor or TV.

* Pairing with smart home devices: Control your smart lights, thermostats, and other compatible devices directly from your Galaxy S24 with the SmartThings app. Create an interconnected home and experience ultimate convenience.

* Printing on the go: Print photos, documents, and web pages directly from your Galaxy S24 to compatible wireless printers without needing a computer.

Personalizing your interface:

Make your Galaxy S24 truly your own by tailoring its interface to your preferences. Here's how to personalize your digital sanctuary:

* Themes: Transform the entire look and feel of your phone with various pre-installed themes or download new ones from the Galaxy Theme Store.

* Wallpapers: Set dynamic wallpapers with animated elements or choose stunning static images to reflect your personality and style.

* Shortcuts: Add shortcuts to your favorite apps, contacts, and functions on the Home screen for

instant access. Long press on app icons or navigate to "Widgets" to customize your shortcuts.

* Widgets: Place informative and interactive widgets on your Home screen for constant updates on weather, news, calendar events, music controls, and more.

* Icon packs: Change the app icon appearance with custom icon packs for a cohesive and personalized visual experience.

1. Setting Up DeX:

* Compatibility check:Ensure your Galaxy S24 model and accessories are compatible with DeX. Most recent flagships and some mid-range models support DeX. You'll need a compatible HDMI cable or adapter depending on your desired setup.

* Wired vs. Wireless: Connect your phone to a monitor or TV via a cable for a stable and lag-free experience. Alternatively, some newer monitors offer wireless DeX connections for added convenience.

* Launching DeX: Simply unlock your phone and connect it to the monitor. DeX should launch automatically. If not, navigate to "Settings" >

"Advanced Features" > "Samsung DeX" and activate it.

2. Connecting Compatible Devices:

* Mouse and keyboard: Enhance your productivity by connecting a Bluetooth or USB mouse and keyboard for a traditional PC-like feel.
* External storage: Expand your storage capacity by connecting a USB flash drive or external hard drive for storing documents and media files directly on DeX.
* Printer: Print documents and photos directly from DeX by connecting a compatible wireless or USB printer.

3. Optimizing the Interface for Productivity:

* Multi-window multitasking: Open multiple apps simultaneously and resize them for efficient

workflow. Drag and drop content between apps for seamless collaboration.

* Taskbar and shortcuts: Pin frequently used apps to the DeX taskbar for quick access. Customize the desktop with widgets and shortcuts for your favorite functions.

* Keyboard shortcuts: Master keyboard shortcuts for DeX-specific actions like switching windows, taking screenshots, and launching apps for even faster navigation.

4. Powerful DeX-Specific Features:

* App mirroring: Use your phone's screen as an additional touchpad or display different content on both screens simultaneously.

* Samsung Remote: Control presentations, browse the web, and navigate DeX using your phone as a remote control.

* Secret DeX features:Discover hidden gems like screen recording, multi-language keyboard support, and custom wallpapers to personalize your DeX experience.

1. Adding and Managing Cards:

* Effortless setup: Learn how to quickly and securely add your credit, debit, loyalty, and gift cards to the Samsung Pay app using your phone's camera or manual entry.
* Card organization: Discover tips for managing multiple cards, setting preferred payment options, and easily switching between them on the fly.
* Emergency card access: Explore options for adding backup cards in case your primary card is lost or stolen, ensuring you're never caught off guard.

2. Configuring Security Settings:

* Pin and biometric authentication: Understand the importance of setting a strong PIN and enabling fingerprint or facial recognition for secure transactions.

* Auto-lock and spending limits: Configure auto-lock features to automatically lock the app after a period of inactivity and set spending limits for added control.

* Notification and transaction alerts: Stay informed about your spending with real-time transaction notifications and keep track of your financial activity.

3. Making Contactless Payments in Various Scenarios:

* Retail stores: Learn how to breeze through checkout lines by making quick and secure contactless payments at compatible stores.

* Public transportation: Discover the convenience of paying for fares on buses, trains, and other public transportation systems using your Galaxy S24.

* Online and in-app purchases: Explore using Samsung Pay for secure online and in-app purchases, eliminating the need for manual card details.

* Sharing bills and sending money: Discover features like Samsung Pay Send, which allows you

to share bills and send money to friends and family directly from your phone.

4. Advanced Features and Rewards:

* Samsung Pay Rewards: Unlock cashback offers and earn reward points while shopping at participating merchants, adding an extra layer of benefit to your everyday transactions.
* Gift cards and coupons: Easily store and manage gift cards and coupons within the Samsung Pay app for quick access and convenient redemption.
* Samsung Pay Mini: Explore using Samsung Pay Mini on compatible wearable devices like Galaxy Watches, allowing you to make contactless payments without even needing your phone.

1. Tracking Your Key Metrics:

* Steps and Activity: Monitor your daily step count, active minutes, and distance covered to understand your overall activity level.

* Workouts: Log your workouts, whether running, cycling, swimming, or hitting the gym, and analyze specific metrics like pace, heart rate, and calories burned.

* Sleep:Track your sleep patterns, including duration, quality, and sleep stages, to gain insights into your sleep health.

* Nutrition: Input your meals and snacks to monitor your calorie intake, macronutrient balance, and water consumption.

* Health Measurements: Monitor key health indicators like blood pressure, weight, oxygen saturation, and stress levels to gain a holistic view of your well-being.

2. Setting Goals and Staying Motivated:

* Personalized goals: Set achievable goals for steps, activity, workouts, sleep, and other metrics based on your fitness level and aspirations.

* Challenges and rewards: Join in-app challenges to compete with friends or the community, earning badges and rewards for staying motivated.

* Insights and recommendations: Get personalized insights and recommendations based on your activity data and progress towards your goals.

* Sharing and social support: Share your progress with friends and family, or join online communities for motivation and encouragement.

3. Advanced Features and Integrations:

* Samsung Galaxy Watch:Pair your Galaxy S24 with a compatible Galaxy Watch for automatic activity tracking, continuous heart rate monitoring, and even advanced sleep analysis.

* Third-party apps: Integrate Samsung Health with popular fitness apps and wearable devices to consolidate your data in one place.

* Health coaching: Access Samsung Health coaching programs for personalized guidance on nutrition, exercise, and overall well-being.

* Health data export: Export your health data to other platforms or share it with your doctor for a more comprehensive medical picture.

1. Accessing Bixby Routines:

- Quick access:Swipe down from the top of your screen to open the Quick Panel and locate the Bixby Routines icon (a blue circle with a gear).
- Settings menu: Alternatively, navigate to Settings > Advanced Features > Bixby Routines to access the app.

2. Creating Custom Routines:

- Tap the "Add routine" button to start crafting your own.
- Choose a trigger: Select a specific event that will initiate your routine, such as a particular time of day, location, app usage, device connection, or battery level.
- Add actions: Decide what actions your phone will perform when the trigger is activated. Choose from options like adjusting settings, opening apps,

playing media, sending messages, or controlling smart home devices.
- Customize further: Give your routine a name, choose an icon, and adjust other settings as desired.

3. Exploring Pre-Designed Routines:

- Tap "Discover" to browse a collection of pre-made routines designed for common scenarios like commuting, working, sleeping, or focusing.
- Review and customize:Explore these routines, personalize them to match your preferences, and activate the ones that suit your lifestyle.

4. Managing Your Routines:

- View and edit: Access your created and discovered routines, toggle them on or off, edit their actions, and adjust their settings as needed.
- Advanced settings: Explore options for sharing routines with others, creating backups, and setting priority levels for multiple routines that might activate simultaneously.

5. Examples of Powerful Routines:

- Good morning routine:Turn on your lights, play your favorite news briefing, and adjust your phone's volume when you wake up.
- Work focus routine:Activate Do Not Disturb mode, launch your productivity apps, and set a timer to remind you to take breaks during work hours.
- Bedtime routine:Enable blue light filter, dim the screen, and play relaxing sounds when you're ready to sleep.
- Driving routine: Automatically launch your navigation app, turn on Bluetooth, and start playing your driving playlist when you connect to your car's Bluetooth.

1. Unveiling Bixby Vision's Powers:

* Translation magic: Point your camera at foreign text and watch it instantly translate before your eyes, breaking down language barriers and empowering global communication.
* Object identification: Discover the names and details of objects around you, from landmarks and statues to plants and even products – satisfying your curiosity and expanding your knowledge.
* QR code wizardry: Forget struggling with tiny codes, simply scan them with Bixby Vision for instant access to websites, contact information, or hidden surprises.
* AR furniture placement: Reimagine your home decor! Visualize how furniture pieces would look in your actual space before committing to a purchase, making informed decisions and preventing buyer's remorse.

2. Fun and Practical Applications:

* Exploring landmarks: Discover historical information and interesting facts about buildings,

monuments, and other landmarks just by pointing your camera at them.

* Shopping made easy: See similar products online while you're out and about, compare prices, and find the perfect item without the hassle of searching.

* Unlocking hidden menus: Certain restaurants and cafes offer secret menus accessible through AR codes scannable with Bixby Vision.

* Learning through AR: Engage in interactive learning experiences, view 3D models of objects, and bring educational materials to life with AR overlays.

3. Getting Started with Bixby Vision:

* Open the Camera app on your Galaxy S24.
* Tap the "Bixby Vision" icon located at the top left corner of the screen.
* Point your camera at the object, text, or QR code you want to interact with.
* Bixby Vision will automatically analyze the image and display relevant information or offer available actions.

4. Tips and Tricks:

* Adjust the focus: Ensure the object or text is in clear focus for accurate recognition.
* Lighting matters: Bright, well-lit environments produce better results.
* Explore additional features: Discover other cool capabilities like scene translator, makeup try-on, and food mode available within Bixby Vision.

1. Connecting and Managing Devices:

* Discover compatible devices: Scan your home network or manually add your smart lights, thermostats, appliances, cameras, and more from a wide range of brands.
* Group and categorize: Organize your devices by room, type, or custom groups for easier control and scene creation.
* Monitor status and control remotely:Check if your lights are on, adjust the thermostat from your office, or lock your doors remotely – all at your fingertips.

2. Creating Powerful Scenes:

* Go beyond individual device control:Craft custom scenes that activate multiple devices with a single tap. Imagine turning on all your living room lights, dimming the lamps, and setting the perfect audio mood for movie night.
* Automation magic: Schedule scenes to trigger automatically based on time, location, or other triggers. Arrive home to a pre-lit and welcoming environment, or have your lights automatically adjust at sunrise and sunset.
* SmartThings Routines: Combine scene activation with Bixby Routines for even more complex automation. Imagine a morning routine that turns on your coffee maker, opens the blinds, and plays your favorite music – all while you're still in bed!

3. Enhanced Security and Monitoring:

* Receive instant alerts: Get notified if your sensors detect motion, smoke, or leaks, giving you peace of mind and the ability to respond quickly to potential emergencies.

* Live camera feeds: Keep an eye on your home anytime, anywhere through your connected cameras. Check on the kids playing outside, see who's at the door, or monitor your pets remotely.

* Customizable security settings: Set and arm security systems from your phone, activate specific lights or sirens in case of an alert, and receive real-time video recordings for evidence.

4. Voice Control and Integration:

* Talk to your home: Use voice assistants like Bixby or Google Assistant to control your smart devices effortlessly. Tell your lights to dim, adjust the thermostat, or check the camera feed – all hands-free!

* Connect with other platforms:Expand your smart home ecosystem by integrating SmartThings with popular platforms like Samsung Connect, Philips Hue, and Nest, bringing all your devices under one intuitive interface.

Chapter 16:Samsung Galaxy S24: AI features and software

The "rewrite" feature on Chat Assist, available with Android 14 and One UI 6.1 on the Galaxy S24 series, offers users a convenient tool within the keyboard interface. This feature is designed to assist users in refining the tone and content of their text or email messages. Here's how you can use the "rewrite" feature:

1. Access Chat Assist: Open your keyboard, and you should find the Chat Assist feature integrated into it.

2. Select Text to Rewrite: Highlight the text you want to modify or rewrite within your message.

3. Activate "Rewrite" Option: Look for the "Rewrite" option in the Chat Assist menu, typically accessible through the keyboard interface.

4. Choose Purpose or Translation:Once you've selected "Rewrite," the tool may offer options to adjust the tone based on the purpose of your message. Additionally, you may have the option to

translate the text into one of the 13 available languages supported by Galaxy AI.

5. Spelling and Grammar Check: The "rewrite" feature may also include a spelling and grammar check to ensure that your message is polished and free of errors.

6. Finalize and Send: After making the desired adjustments, you can finalize the rewritten text and proceed to send your message.

This functionality aims to enhance the user experience by providing a quick and easy way to tailor messages for different contexts, ensuring effective communication. Whether you need to adjust the tone, translate the text, or simply refine your message's language, the "rewrite" feature in Chat Assist on the Galaxy S24 series aims to make common smartphone tasks more convenient and powerful.

The mentioned passage doesn't specifically describe a "rewrite" feature, but based on the context, it seems that the overall capabilities of the Galaxy S24, particularly with Galaxy AI, involve advanced functionalities that can enhance and modify various types of content. Here's an interpretation of what a "rewrite" feature could entail in this context:

The "rewrite" feature on the Galaxy S24, powered by Galaxy AI, might allow users to dynamically modify and enhance different types of content. This could involve adjusting the tone and language of written messages, transcribing and summarizing spoken conversations, and even transforming handwritten or typed notes for better clarity and organization.

Potential functionalities of the "rewrite" feature:

1. Text Transformation: Users could rewrite and refine the content of messages, emails, or notes directly within the device. This might involve adjusting the tone, language style, or even translating text into different languages seamlessly.

2. Voice Transcription Enhancement: In conjunction with the Transcribe Assist feature, the "rewrite"

function could help improve the accuracy and clarity of voice transcriptions. Users might have the ability to edit and refine transcribed content, especially in noisy environments.

3. Note Organization and Enhancement: The "rewrite" feature may extend to the Notes app, allowing users to automatically reformat, summarize, or translate typed text. Additionally, it could assist in straightening handwritten notes for better legibility.

4. Web Content Modification: Users might be able to use the "rewrite" feature within the Samsung Internet browser (Browsing Assist) to quickly make long articles more readable, summarize content, or translate it into different languages.

Chapter 17: Samsung Galaxy S24: Performance

The choice of processor in the Galaxy S24 and Galaxy S24 Plus varies depending on the region of purchase. Customers in the United States will receive models equipped with the Snapdragon 8 Gen 3 for Galaxy chip, similar to the Galaxy S24 Ultra. On the other hand, customers outside the United States, including the U.K., will find the Samsung Exynos 2400 for Galaxy chip in their devices.

While the Snapdragon-equipped S24 models are anticipated to deliver top-notch phone performance, there is a historical concern regarding Exynos chips, which have been perceived to offer lower performance compared to their Snapdragon counterparts. This raises considerations for buyers outside the U.S., as they may be concerned about potentially receiving a device with less optimal performance.

Moving on to other specifications, the baseline configuration for the Galaxy S24 includes 8GB of RAM and 128GB of storage, which some may find a bit conservative. However, users have the option to upgrade to a more capacious 256GB storage variant. The Galaxy S24 Plus, on the other hand, comes with a more generous 12GB of RAM and 256GB of storage as the default configuration, with the option to further expand storage to 512GB for users with higher storage needs.

Chapter 18: Samsung Galaxy S24: Battery and charging

Samsung has increased the battery capacities for both the Galaxy S24 and the Galaxy S24 Plus. The Galaxy S24 now boasts a 4,000 mAh battery, a bump from the S23's 3,900 mAh, while the S24 Plus features a 4,900 mAh battery, up from the S23 Plus's 4,700 mAh.

These batteries are powered by the same charging systems as their Galaxy S23 counterparts. The standard charging for the base S24 model remains at 25W, with Samsung asserting that it can charge the phone to 50% in 30 minutes. While this charging speed might be considered moderate compared to some competing phones, it aligns with the charging rates of the latest devices from Apple and Google.

On the other hand, the 45W charging capability is exclusive to the Plus model and higher. Samsung claims that it can charge the Galaxy S24 Plus to 65% in half an hour. While slightly improved, it still falls within a similar charging timeframe compared to other flagship smartphones, showcasing a notable but not exceptionally fast charging speed.

Chapter 19: Samsung Galaxy S24: Outlook

The Galaxy S24 and Galaxy S24 Plus incorporate familiar hardware in many aspects, but notable upgrades, coupled with the Galaxy AI package, position them as strong contenders against the Google Pixel 8 series in terms of AI features and the iPhone 15 series in photography capabilities and overall computing power.

Your appreciation for these phones is likely to hinge on how much utility you derive from the advanced AI features. With enhancements in camera functionality, note-taking, translation, and transcription options, there's a good chance that at least one of these features will capture your interest.

The primary decision then revolves around whether you prioritize the added value offered by the more affordable base Galaxy S24 or the larger size, increased battery capacity (presumably resulting in longer battery life), and faster charging speeds of the Galaxy S24 Plus.

While comprehensive reviews of the Galaxy S24 and Galaxy S24 Plus are forthcoming, the current assessment suggests significant upgrades from the Galaxy S23, even if many of these changes aren't immediately evident from the exterior. Stay tuned for our detailed reviews for a more in-depth evaluation of these devices.

Chapter 20: Samsung Galaxy S24: Design and display

The design of the Galaxy S24 closely resembles its predecessor, the S23, featuring a flat screen and back panel joined by metal side rails. However, the S24 introduces a unibody-like design, seamlessly blending the separate panels for a refined and well-built appearance. While the Galaxy S23 was already perceived as a sophisticated device, the S24 takes it a step further.

It's worth noting that the frame of the S24 is crafted from aluminum, unlike the titanium used in the Ultra model. Additionally, the new Gorilla Armor Glass, which protects the Ultra's display, is absent in the base and Plus models. Nevertheless, both phones come equipped with the robust Gorilla Glass Victus 2 and share the benefit of an IP68 rating, ensuring resilience against water splashes and submersion.

Examining the display, the base Galaxy S24 features a larger 6.2-inch OLED display with slimmer bezels compared to the S23. The Galaxy S24 Plus has also increased its screen size from 6.6 inches to 6.7 inches. Despite the larger screens, the phones maintain a similar overall size while offering more display space, contributing to improved screen-to-body ratios. The screens boast a high brightness of up to 2,600 nits, ensuring visibility even in harsh lighting conditions.

Both models receive an upgrade to a full 1-120Hz adaptive refresh rate, which was previously exclusive to the Ultra model. The S24 Plus additionally features a QHD+ display, providing more detail on its larger panel.

Lastly, the color selection offers four choices for both the Galaxy S24 and Galaxy S24 Plus. Notable options include Cobalt Violet, with a rich purple tone, and Amber Yellow, which appears pale under bright light but has an appealingly cheerful hue. Onyx Black and Marble Gray round out the selection with sophisticated and smart-looking options.

www.ingramcontent.com/pod-product-compliance
Lightning Source LLC
LaVergne TN
LVHW051607050326
832903LV00033B/4392